Christian Faith and Mental Health

Stability in the Church Community

by

Dr. David K. Ewen

Minister

ISBN: 9798872277071
Imprint: Independently published by Enterprise College

Cover art by Emma Simpson via Unsplash

Dr. David K. Ewen

Cover art by Emma Simpson via Unsplash

About the Book

The correlation between Christian faith and mental health has been a subject of intricate exploration and discussion. Within the teachings of Christianity, fundamental principles like forgiveness and gratitude are believed to wield substantial influence over mental well-being. Christianity emphasizes the significance of forgiveness—both seeking it from God and extending it to others. This practice holds potential transformative effects on mental health, as harboring grudges and resentment can breed bitterness, anger, and anxiety. By embracing forgiveness, individuals can experience liberation and peace, shedding negative emotions and redirecting focus towards personal growth.

Moreover, gratitude stands as another pivotal principle in Christianity with the potential to positively impact mental well-being. Cultivating gratitude, acknowledging blessings, and expressing thanks for life's positives can foster contentment and happiness. Studies indicate that individuals who regularly practice gratitude exhibit lower levels of stress, anxiety, and depression.

Christian faith, in offering a sense of hope and purpose, provides a framework for understanding life's challenges and discovering meaning in difficult circumstances. Particularly in times of adversity, faith can provide solace, comfort, and resilience, serving as a guiding light.

However, the relationship between Christian faith and mental health is multifaceted. While faith can serve as a source of strength and support, it's crucial to recognize its limitations. Faith is not a cure-all for all mental health issues. Individuals may still require professional help, such as therapy or medication, to address specific conditions. Additionally, faith can sometimes be misinterpreted or misapplied, leading to harmful practices or unrealistic expectations.

Therefore, approaching the association between Christian faith and mental health demands a balanced perspective. Acknowledging the potential benefits of faith while recognizing the need for comprehensive care is essential. Integrating the teachings of Christianity with evidence-based practices enables individuals to cultivate a holistic approach to mental well-being that incorporates both faith and science.

About the Author

Dr. David K. Ewen is an extraordinary individual whose professional journey embodies a unique intersection of ministry, academia, and mental health advocacy. As an ordained minister and accomplished international university professor at Global Studies University, he brings a wealth of knowledge and experience to the challenging field of mental health, particularly among marginalized communities.

Dr. Ewen's dedication extends beyond conventional academic boundaries. His commitment to addressing mental health issues among incarcerated individuals and the homeless community showcases his compassionate spirit and desire to serve those in need. Working within these often-overlooked populations requires a deep understanding of the complexities surrounding mental health challenges and social disparities.

Beyond his roles in academia and ministry, Dr. Ewen's contributions as an author, speaker, and podcaster highlight his commitment to raising awareness and initiating conversations about mental health. His written works likely offer insightful perspectives, drawing from his extensive experience and expertise in working with these vulnerable communities. Through speaking engagements and podcast discussions, he likely engages audiences, fostering dialogue and understanding about mental health issues that affect diverse populations.

Dr. Ewen's multidimensional approach to mental health, blending academia, ministry, advocacy, and media outreach, underscores his comprehensive and holistic approach to addressing mental health concerns. His work exemplifies the importance of integrating various disciplines to create meaningful change and support for those grappling with mental health challenges in underserved communities.

In essence, Dr. David K. Ewen's impactful contributions in academia, ministry, and mental health advocacy signify a passionate commitment to improving the lives of marginalized individuals. His multifaceted approach, coupled with his dedication as an author, speaker, and podcaster, serves as an inspiration in the collective effort to foster understanding, compassion, and support for those facing mental health struggles among society's most vulnerable populations.

Dr. David K. Ewen

Minister

Table of Contents

Chapter 1: Forgiveness and Mental Well-being

Central to Christianity, the concept of forgiveness is a powerful and transformative practice that involves releasing resentment and extending compassion to those who have wronged us. It is a fundamental aspect of the Christian faith, emphasizing the importance of letting go of anger and embracing love and understanding. By forgiving others, we not only free ourselves from the burden of holding onto grudges, but we also open the door to spiritual growth and healing.

Forgiveness has a profound impact on mental health as well. When we harbor resentment and hold onto negative emotions, it can have detrimental effects on our well-being. The accumulation of anger, bitterness, and resentment can lead to stress, anxiety, and even depression. However, by practicing forgiveness, we can prevent these negative emotions from festering within us.

The act of forgiveness can be liberating and bring about a sense of peace. It allows us to let go of the past and move forward with a lighter heart. When we forgive, we release ourselves from the chains of anger and resentment, and we create space for compassion and understanding. This newfound liberation can have a profound impact on our mental well-being, promoting a sense of inner peace and contentment.

Furthermore, forgiveness is not only beneficial for the individual, but it also has the potential to foster healthier relationships and communities. When we extend forgiveness to others, it opens the door for reconciliation and healing. The act of forgiveness is a powerful tool that can bring about positive change in both personal and interpersonal dynamics. It allows for the restoration of trust and the rebuilding of relationships that may have been damaged by past hurts. By choosing to forgive, we release ourselves from the burden of resentment and anger, and create space for understanding and empathy. This shift in perspective can lead to a deeper level of connection and compassion with others.

In the context of communities, forgiveness plays a vital role in promoting harmony and unity. When individuals practice forgiveness, it creates an environment that is conducive to empathy, compassion, and understanding. It encourages people to let go of grudges and conflicts, and instead focus on finding common ground and working towards shared goals. In forgiving others, we acknowledge our own imperfections and recognize the inherent humanity in others. This recognition fosters a sense of belonging and togetherness, strengthening the social fabric of our communities.

Moreover, forgiveness has the power to break the cycle of hurt and retaliation that often perpetuates conflict. When we choose forgiveness, we disrupt the negative patterns of behavior and replace them with a more positive and constructive approach. Rather than seeking revenge or holding onto negativity, forgiveness allows us to move forward and create meaningful change. It enables us to learn from our experiences and grow as individuals and as a collective.

Furthermore, forgiveness has been shown to have numerous health benefits, both mental and physical. Research indicates that holding onto grudges and harboring feelings of anger and resentment can have detrimental effects on our well-being. However, when we choose forgiveness, we experience a sense of relief, peace, and emotional healing. This can lead to reduced stress levels, improved mental health, and increased overall life satisfaction. Additionally, forgiveness has been associated with lower blood pressure, reduced risk of heart disease, and improved immune function.

In conclusion, forgiveness is not only a personal journey but also a powerful force that has the potential to transform relationships and communities. By practicing forgiveness, we create an environment that is conducive to empathy, compassion, and unity, promoting overall well-being within our communities. It allows for reconciliation, healing, and the restoration of trust. The act of forgiveness breaks the cycle of hurt and retaliation, fostering positive change and growth. Moreover, forgiveness has significant health benefits, benefiting both our mental and physical well-being. By embracing forgiveness, we can create a more harmonious and compassionate world for ourselves and future generations.

Chapter 2: Gratitude and Its Effects

Gratitude stands as a cornerstone within Christian teachings, embodying a profound acknowledgment and appreciation for life's blessings. Its significance extends far beyond a mere attitude; it serves as a transformative force, encouraging believers to perceive the world through a lens of thankfulness and abundance.

In the tapestry of Christian faith, gratitude is woven intricately, fostering not just appreciation but a deep recognition of the inherent goodness and richness in one's life. The act of cultivating a grateful heart has garnered significant attention in psychological studies, unveiling a multitude of benefits that extend to mental, emotional, and spiritual well-being.

One of the remarkable facets of gratitude is its power to reduce stress, elevate happiness levels, and amplify overall life satisfaction. When individuals consciously express gratitude, they pivot their focus from scarcity to abundance, thereby fostering a profound sense of contentment and fulfillment. This shift in perspective catalyzes a ripple effect, altering how one perceives circumstances, relationships, and experiences.

Within the Christian context, gratitude becomes a beacon of hope and resilience in times of adversity. Amidst life's trials and tribulations, the practice of gratitude empowers individuals to discover blessings even amidst challenges. It becomes a transformative tool, allowing believers to navigate hardships with a sense of grace and steadfast faith. Through the active practice of gratitude, Christians fortify their mental resilience, finding strength and solace in the acknowledgment of blessings, no matter how modest they may seem.

Beyond the realms of Christian teachings, gratitude transcends religious boundaries, resonating as a universal practice that has the potential to usher profound positive changes in one's life. It serves as a gentle reminder, prompting individuals to pause and be grateful for the often overlooked blessings, fostering humility and a deeper appreciation for life's wonders.

The essence of gratitude goes beyond the mere act of saying "thank you" for what one has received. It encompasses a deeper understanding and practice of cultivating an attitude of continuous appreciation—a state of being that permeates everyday life. Whether it is Christians or individuals of diverse beliefs, embracing gratitude as a way of living brings about numerous benefits. Firstly, cultivating a positive mindset becomes second nature when one chooses to focus on the things they are grateful for. It shifts the perspective from dwelling on what is lacking to recognizing the abundance that exists. This positive mindset not only enhances one's overall well-being but also influences their interactions with others, creating a ripple effect of positivity.

Secondly, gratitude helps individuals embrace life's fluctuations with resilience. It is inevitable that life will present both ups and downs, but a grateful heart finds strength in the face of adversity. Rather than succumbing to despair, individuals who practice gratitude are able to find silver linings, lessons, and opportunities for growth even in challenging circumstances. This resilience allows them to bounce back stronger, fostering personal development and self-improvement.

Lastly, gratitude enables individuals to find joy in the richness of their experiences. By recognizing and appreciating the blessings and beauty that surround them, individuals are able to derive greater satisfaction from the simplest of moments. Gratitude encourages mindfulness, as individuals become more attuned to the present moment and the wonders it holds. This heightened awareness allows them to fully engage with their surroundings, fostering a sense of awe and wonder. As a result, life becomes more vibrant, meaningful, and fulfilling.

In conclusion, the essence of gratitude lies in more than just expressing gratitude through words. It is a way of life, a continuous attitude of appreciation that permeates every aspect of one's existence. By embracing gratitude, individuals, regardless of their religious beliefs, can cultivate a positive mindset, embrace life's fluctuations with resilience, and find joy in the richness of their experiences. Gratitude is a transformative practice that enhances well-being, strengthens relationships, and brings about a deeper sense of contentment and fulfillment.

Chapter 3: Positive Impacts Backed by Research

Christian communities often grapple with the intersection of mental health and spirituality, sometimes leaning towards attributing mental illness solely to spiritual causes such as sin or lack of faith. However, empirical evidence suggests a more nuanced relationship between Christian faith and mental health. While elements within Christian practices can significantly benefit individuals with mental health challenges, it's crucial to avoid over-spiritualizing these issues and adopt a more holistic approach.

Research has demonstrated that adherence to Christian principles correlates with increased happiness, resilience, and a reduced propensity for substance abuse or suicidal tendencies. However, it's essential to emphasize that experiencing mental illness does not imply spiritual immaturity or divine punishment. Despite some perceptions within Christian circles associating mental illness with spiritual factors like sin, demons, or insufficient faith, a holistic model integrating spiritual, psychological, and social aspects is crucial for addressing mental health issues effectively.

Faith-based interventions have shown promise in alleviating depressive symptoms and fostering a stronger sense of connection. Nevertheless, the belief that mental illness is solely a spiritual matter can be detrimental, deterring individuals from seeking necessary medical or psychological assistance. Understanding that mental health disorders have multifaceted causes, including genetics, environment, and neurochemistry, is crucial.

While spirituality can offer solace and strength, it should complement, not replace, professional treatment.

Christian communities must cultivate an atmosphere of empathy and support for those facing mental health challenges. Educating members about mental health combats misconceptions and encourages compassion. Integrating a holistic approach that acknowledges spiritual, psychological, and social dimensions can fortify the support system within these communities.

Furthermore, individuals grappling with mental illness within Christian circles should not face judgment or stigma. It is important to recognize that mental health struggles are not indicative of one's faith or spiritual maturity. Just as physical ailments do not define a person's commitment to their beliefs, mental health challenges should not be used as a measure of one's devotion to Christianity. It is crucial for Christian communities to create an atmosphere of acceptance and understanding, where individuals can feel safe and supported in seeking help for their mental health concerns. By nurturing this culture of acceptance, Christian communities can actively promote mental health and well-being.

Instead of perpetuating judgment or stigmatizing those with mental illness, Christian communities should encourage individuals to seek help without fear of shame or misunderstanding. Mental health issues are not a sign of weakness or moral failing, but rather a complex interplay of biological, psychological, and social factors. Just as Christians are called to love and care for their neighbors, it is equally important to extend that love and care to those who are struggling with mental health challenges.

By fostering an environment that embraces acceptance and understanding, Christian communities can play a significant role in promoting mental health and well-being. This can be achieved through education and awareness campaigns within the church, providing resources and support groups for individuals and families affected by mental illness, and training church leaders to recognize the signs of mental health struggles and respond with compassion and empathy.

Moreover, Christian communities can actively engage in conversations surrounding mental health and faith, breaking down the stigma and misconceptions that often surround this topic. By openly discussing mental health and sharing personal experiences, individuals within the Christian community can inspire hope and healing for those who are facing similar challenges. Furthermore, Christian leaders and influencers can use their platforms to address mental health issues, providing guidance and encouragement to those who may be silently suffering.

Chapter 4: Support Networks Within Christian Communities

The framework provided by Christian faith extends far beyond religious beliefs and practices. Within faith communities, there exists a unique and powerful support network that significantly impacts mental health. These communities serve as safe spaces where individuals can find solace, support, understanding, and guidance, all of which contribute immensely to their overall mental well-being.

The power of these support networks lies in their ability to foster a sense of belonging and connection. They enable individuals to share their struggles, fears, and joys with others who genuinely understand and empathize with their experiences. This sense of community creates a supportive environment that alleviates feelings of isolation and loneliness, which are often associated with mental health issues.

In these faith communities, individuals are encouraged to lean on their faith, find hope in times of adversity, and develop resilience in the face of challenges. The belief in a higher power provides comfort and reassurance, offering a sense of purpose and meaning in life, even in the midst of difficulties. The teachings of Christian faith emphasize compassion, love, forgiveness, and acceptance, creating an environment where individuals are encouraged to extend these virtues towards themselves and others, thus promoting a positive and nurturing atmosphere for mental health.

Faith, hope, and resilience intertwine deeply within these communities, showcasing the profound and lasting positive effects of Christian faith on mental health. The encouragement to cultivate these virtues not only aids in managing stress and adversity but also strengthens one's psychological well-being. The support and guidance provided within faith communities empower individuals to navigate life's challenges with a sense of purpose and optimism.

Moreover, the rituals, prayers, and spiritual practices within these communities offer avenues for introspection, mindfulness, and meditation. These practices can foster inner peace and emotional stability, contributing to mental clarity and overall well-being. The communal worship and participation in religious ceremonies often generate feelings of joy, gratitude, and serenity, which are beneficial for mental health.

Additionally, Christian faith communities often offer counseling services, support groups, and resources tailored to addressing mental health concerns. This proactive approach to mental health care further demonstrates the holistic support provided within these environments.

Christian faith communities, alongside various religious institutions, often serve as foundational pillars for individuals seeking solace, guidance, and a sense of belonging. Within these communities, there exists a unique blend of faith-based principles, communal support structures, and psychological insights that contribute significantly to the overall mental and emotional well-being of their members.

Firstly, Christian faith communities typically offer a set of guiding principles and beliefs that can provide a sense of purpose, hope, and resilience in challenging times. These principles often include teachings on love, compassion, forgiveness, and the value of community. They offer a framework for understanding and navigating life's difficulties, fostering a sense of meaning and direction that can be instrumental in supporting mental health.

Secondly, one of the defining features of Christian faith communities is their emphasis on communal support and fellowship. Members often come together regularly for worship, prayer, and various activities, fostering a sense of belonging and interconnectedness. This communal support network can serve as a source of encouragement, empathy, and practical assistance during times of hardship, loneliness, or distress. The social connections within these communities can mitigate feelings of isolation and provide a sense of solidarity, which is crucial for mental well-being.

Furthermore, many Christian faith communities integrate psychological insights and support into their pastoral care. Pastors, clergy, and religious leaders often receive training that includes elements of counseling and psychology, enabling them to offer guidance and support rooted in both faith-based wisdom and psychological understanding. This combination allows for a holistic approach to mental health care, addressing spiritual, emotional, and psychological needs.

By integrating these elements, Christian faith communities contribute to nurturing a sense of wholeness and resilience among their members. They provide spaces where individuals can openly discuss their struggles, seek guidance without fear of judgment, and find strength in shared faith and experiences. This nurturing environment encourages personal growth, emotional healing, and the development of coping mechanisms to navigate life's challenges.

Chapter 5: Diverse Perspectives and Balancing Support

Understanding mental health within Christianity requires a nuanced appreciation for the diverse perspectives that exist within this faith. Christianity is not a monolith but a tapestry of beliefs, practices, and interpretations across various denominations. These differences extend to how mental health is perceived and addressed within Christian communities.

Scriptural interpretations significantly influence viewpoints on mental health among different Christian denominations. Some emphasize a reliance on prayer and faith as the primary means of healing, viewing mental health challenges through a spiritual lens. For these groups, spiritual practices and communal support play integral roles in managing mental well-being.

On the other hand, certain denominations advocate for seeking professional help alongside spiritual guidance. They recognize the value of evidence-based therapies, medication, and counseling provided by mental health professionals in addressing mental health concerns. This perspective acknowledges that mental illnesses are multifaceted and often necessitate specialized care beyond solely spiritual interventions.

Acknowledging and respecting these diverse perspectives within Christianity enriches discussions about mental health and prevents oversimplification or generalizations. It allows for a more comprehensive understanding of the complexities individuals face when navigating mental health challenges within their faith context.

Striking a balance between religious and professional help is essential in addressing mental health issues within Christian communities. Faith-based support systems offer valuable comfort, guidance, and a sense of belonging, promoting emotional resilience through prayer, meditation, and religious practices. These spiritual tools can significantly aid individuals in their mental health journey, offering strength and solace.

However, it's crucial to recognize that mental health concerns often necessitate professional intervention. Trained mental health professionals possess the expertise to diagnose, treat, and provide evidence-based therapies for mental illnesses. Seeking professional help aligns with the Christian principle of stewardship—responsibly caring for one's well-being by utilizing the resources and expertise available.

The integration of faith-based practices and professional interventions in addressing mental health needs represents a holistic and inclusive approach that acknowledges the interconnectedness of spiritual and mental well-being. This balanced approach is grounded in the understanding that individuals possess diverse backgrounds, belief systems, and personal experiences that influence their healing journey.

Faith-based practices encompass a wide spectrum of spiritual traditions, rituals, prayer, meditation, scripture study, worship, and community engagement. For many individuals within Christian communities, these practices hold significant importance in nurturing their spiritual health. They provide a sense of purpose, hope, comfort, and guidance during challenging times, offering a framework for understanding life's complexities.

Simultaneously, professional interventions such as counseling, therapy, psychiatric care, and evidence-based treatments offer specialized expertise in addressing mental health concerns. These interventions utilize psychological theories, therapeutic techniques, and medical knowledge to support individuals in managing conditions, navigating emotional struggles, and fostering resilience.

The amalgamation of these approaches does not prioritize one over the other but rather acknowledges their complementary nature. It respects the autonomy of individuals to navigate their mental health journey by integrating faith-based practices alongside evidence-based professional interventions based on their unique needs and preferences.

This balanced approach within Christian communities cultivates an environment of acceptance, understanding, and support. It encourages open dialogue about mental health concerns without stigma or judgment, allowing individuals to seek help without fear of reproach. It emphasizes the importance of community, fostering a network where individuals can find comfort, encouragement, and guidance from fellow believers and professionals alike.

Moreover, embracing this holistic approach fosters healing on multiple levels. It acknowledges that mental health struggles can be complex and multifaceted, requiring comprehensive care that addresses the spiritual, emotional, psychological, and physical aspects of an individual's well-being. By integrating faith-based practices and professional interventions, individuals are empowered to engage in a healing process that acknowledges their whole selves.

Compassion, empathy, and grace are integral components of this approach, encouraging a non-judgmental and supportive atmosphere within Christian communities. It promotes a deeper understanding of one another's struggles and encourages walking alongside each other in times of need.

In summary, the integration of faith-based practices and professional interventions in addressing mental health needs within Christian communities represents a holistic, person-centered approach. It recognizes the interconnectedness of spiritual and mental well-being, fostering healing, understanding, and compassion while providing a supportive environment where individuals can seek comprehensive care for their holistic health needs.

Chapter 6: Challenging Stigma and Future Research Directions

Addressing the stigma surrounding mental health within Christian communities is a crucial endeavor that aligns with the core teachings of love, compassion, and care espoused by Christianity. Despite these teachings, misconceptions and misunderstanding about mental health persist, creating barriers for individuals seeking support within their faith communities. By actively confronting and dismantling this stigma, we can foster understanding, empathy, and supportive environments where those grappling with mental health challenges can find acceptance and assistance.

Dispelling misconceptions is a primary reason for combating stigma within Christian communities. Erroneous beliefs linking mental health issues to personal weakness or a lack of faith contribute to feelings of shame and guilt. These misconceptions inhibit individuals from acknowledging their struggles or seeking the necessary help. Raising awareness and providing education within Christian contexts can correct these misunderstandings, encouraging a more empathetic and informed perspective on mental health issues.

Encouraging empathy is another critical aspect of addressing stigma. Christian teachings emphasize love and care for others, yet the stigma surrounding mental health often leads to judgment and isolation. Fostering empathy cultivates an environment where individuals can openly share their struggles without fear of condemnation, nurturing a supportive community where mutual understanding and compassion prevail.

Creating supportive environments within Christian communities is pivotal for those dealing with mental health challenges. The isolation and overwhelming nature of such struggles can be alleviated by establishing safe spaces where individuals feel accepted and supported. This supportive atmosphere encourages individuals to seek help, access appropriate resources, and embark on a journey toward recovery within the embrace of their faith community.

Additionally, identifying areas for further research is essential to advance knowledge at the intersection of faith and mental health within Christian contexts. Research enables a deeper understanding of the unique challenges faced by individuals in these communities and facilitates the development of targeted interventions. Evaluating the effectiveness of these interventions through research ensures that the support offered to those grappling with mental health issues is evidence-based and tailored to their specific needs.

Addressing the stigma around mental health in Christian communities is a complex but crucial task that requires a comprehensive strategy. Here's a more detailed exploration of the steps involved:

Firstly, combating this stigma involves educating everyone within these communities. Offering accurate, science-based information about mental health conditions—such as their causes, symptoms, and treatments—is essential. This education equips clergy members, leaders, and the congregation to recognize signs of mental health issues, provide proper support, and encourage seeking professional help when necessary.

Secondly, fostering a culture of empathy and understanding is key. Encouraging open discussions about mental health challenges within Christian groups breaks down barriers. Sharing personal stories of hardship and recovery diminishes stigma and builds empathy among members. Creating a safe, non-judgmental environment where individuals can express their struggles freely is vital.

Thirdly, establishing supportive spaces within Christian settings means providing resources and support systems for those dealing with mental health challenges. This could involve forming support groups, offering counseling services, or collaborating with mental health professionals or organizations. Churches can provide a sense of community and belonging to those facing mental health issues, emphasizing that seeking help aligns with Christian values.

Moreover, supporting mental health research within these communities can lead to a better understanding of how faith and mental health intersect. Working together with mental health professionals and researchers allows for evidence-based practices to be combined with spiritual beliefs. This collaboration helps in developing effective strategies to address mental health challenges within Christian contexts.

By putting these strategies into action, Christian communities can create inclusive and supportive environments that reflect the core values of love, compassion, and support. Embracing the complexity of mental health challenges while integrating faith-based perspectives allows for a holistic approach that considers the spiritual, emotional, and psychological aspects of individuals' well-being.

Ultimately, this multifaceted approach aims to break down barriers, offer support, and encourage individuals within Christian communities to seek help without feeling ashamed or fearful. It fosters an environment where mental health challenges are met with compassion, understanding, and appropriate care.

Chapter 7: Conclusion

The intersection of Christian faith and mental health represents a complex landscape that necessitates comprehensive consideration of various facets, including diverse perspectives, the integration of religious and professional support, efforts to combat stigma, and the pursuit of further research. Within Christian communities, individuals grappling with mental health often encounter distinct challenges that warrant a nuanced approach.

Christianity, for many, serves as a source of comfort, hope, and resilience amid mental health struggles. Prayer, engagement with scripture, and the supportive embrace of a spiritual community often offer solace and strength. Nevertheless, acknowledging the intricate nature of mental health issues is imperative. These challenges frequently require specialized professional assistance. Achieving a balance between religious and professional support is essential to ensure individuals receive holistic care that addresses both spiritual and psychological needs.

Moreover, the stigma surrounding mental health within Christian communities can impede individuals from seeking help or discussing their struggles openly. Combatting this stigma is crucial. By fostering understanding and acceptance, environments that encourage open dialogue and support can be cultivated. Creating such spaces within Christian contexts is vital for individuals to feel empowered to seek assistance without fear of judgment or condemnation.

Further research is fundamental in deepening our comprehension of how religious beliefs and practices intersect with mental health. This exploration can illuminate effective interventions and support systems tailored to individuals navigating mental health challenges within Christian communities. Understanding the intricate dynamics between faith and mental health will pave the way for more targeted and impactful approaches in providing support and care.

The integration of mental health care within Christian communities represents a pivotal step toward fostering comprehensive well-being. Embracing mental health within these communities involves acknowledging the interconnectedness of spiritual, emotional, and psychological aspects of human experience.

Central to this approach is the recognition that mental health is not separate from one's faith but an integral part of a person's overall well-being. By embracing this viewpoint, Christian communities can create spaces that honor the complexity of human existence, providing support that is inclusive of both spiritual and psychological needs.

The goal is to cultivate an environment where individuals feel safe and supported, free from the stigma often associated with seeking professional mental health assistance. The fear of being judged or labeled as lacking faith can hinder individuals from seeking the help they need. Therefore, these communities strive to eliminate such barriers, encouraging open discussions about mental health, and emphasizing the importance of seeking professional assistance when necessary.

By adopting a holistic approach that intertwines faith and mental health, individuals are empowered to navigate life's challenges with a sense of purpose and resilience. It involves recognizing that spirituality can be a source of strength and hope, complementing evidence-based mental health interventions. This integration does not seek to replace professional help but aims to complement it, acknowledging that spiritual beliefs and practices can play a significant role in one's healing journey.

Leaders within Christian communities play a crucial role in fostering this understanding and creating supportive environments. Education, awareness campaigns, and incorporating mental health discussions into sermons or teachings can help dismantle misconceptions and encourage a more open dialogue about mental health.

Ultimately, the aim is to create a culture of compassion, acceptance, and support within Christian communities, where individuals feel empowered to seek both spiritual solace and professional assistance without fear of judgment. This comprehensive approach to mental health not only benefits individuals but also strengthens the community as a whole by nurturing healthier, more resilient members who can contribute positively to their families, churches, and society at large.

Cover art by Emma Simpson via Unsplash

Dr. David K. Ewen

Minister

Christian Faith and Mental Health

Stability in the Church Community

by

Dr. David K. Ewen

Minister